A TRUE BOOK™

WHAT BANKS DO WITH MONEY

LOANS, INTEREST RATES, INVESTMENTS...AND MUCH MORE!

Janet Liu and Melinda Liu

Children's Press®
An imprint of Scholastic Inc.

Content Consultant
Dr. Marie A. Bussing
Emeriti Faculty, Romain College of Business
University of Southern Indiana

Library of Congress Cataloging-in-Publication Data
Names: Liu, Janet, author. | Liu, Melinda (Children's author), author.
Title: What banks do with money: loans, interest rates, investments . . . and much more! / by Janet and
   Melinda Liu.
Description: First edition. | New York, NY: Children's Press, an imprint of Scholastic, Inc., 2024. | Series: A
   true book: money! | Includes bibliographical references and index. | Audience: Ages 8–10. | Audience:
   Grades 4–6. | Summary: "A series to build strong financial habits early on in life! How can I make
   money? What is inflation? What is the difference between a debit card and a credit card? Economics—
   and more specifically, money-play such a large role in our lives. Yet there are many mysteries and
   misconceptions surrounding the basic concepts of finance and smart money management. This A
   True Book series offers students the know-how they'll need to start on the road to financial literacy—a
   crucial skill for today's world. Interesting information is presented in a fun, friendly way—and in the
   simplest terms possible—which will enable students to build strong financial habits early on in life.
   Understanding how banks work—as well as the basics of loans and investments—are just two critical
   financial literacy skills that all kids should have. Did you know that banks use customers' deposits to
   make loans to other customers? Or that the Federal Reserve is the central bank of the United States?
   Learn all this and more in What Banks Do with Money—a book that introduces kids to banking."—
   Provided by publisher.
Identifiers: LCCN 2022054131 (print) | LCCN 2022054132 (ebook) | ISBN 9781339004969 (library binding) |
   ISBN 9781339004976 (paperback) | ISBN 9781339004983 (ebk)
Subjects: LCSH: Banks and banking—Juvenile literature. | Bank accounts—Juvenile literature. | Loans—
   Juvenile literature. | BISAC: JUVENILE NONFICTION / Concepts / Money | JUVENILE NONFICTION / General
Classification: LCC HG1609 .L58 2023 (print) | LCC HG1609 (ebook) | DDC 332.1—dc23/eng/20221206
LC record available at https://lccn.loc.gov/2022054131
LC ebook record available at https://lccn.loc.gov/2022054132

10 9 8 7 6 5 4 3 2 1   24 25 26 27 28

Printed in China 62
First edition, 2024

Design by Kathleen Petelinsek
Series produced by Spooky Cheetah Press

Find the Truth!

Everything you are about to read is true *except* for one of the sentences on this page.

Which one is **TRUE**?

T or F Banks earn money by making loans.

T or F Stocks are low-risk investments.

Find the answers in this book.

What's in This Book?

This is an old
advertisement for
bonds. Bonds are a
type of investment.

Customers can use a deposit slip to add money to their bank accounts.

The **BIG** Truth

How Do Banks Make Money?

3 Investments

Many people use their phones for banking.

INTRODUCTION

Even if you've never been inside a bank, you've probably seen one—or two or three—in your town. And maybe you've wondered just what, exactly, a bank does. For one thing, **a bank is a safe place** for people to keep their money.

Bank vaults hold money, documents, and other valuables. They are tough enough to withstand a nuclear blast.

A bank is also a place where **someone can come for a loan**. When a bank provides a loan for someone to buy a home, go to college, or start a business, it is helping the community. It is also helping the nation's **economy** grow.

The World Bank is an international financial institution. It provides assistance to developing countries around the globe.

The Industrial and Commercial Bank of China is the largest bank in the world.

Bank tellers help customers with deposits and other banking needs.

Money in the Bank

Not all banks are the same. Some banks have branches all over the country. Others operate only in certain regions. Some banks work with families and individuals. Others work with businesses and large institutions—like the government. However, all banks are businesses. They rely on customers—which includes people who **deposit** money and people who borrow money—to make money.

Retail and Commercial Banks

Your family probably uses a retail bank. Retail banks are also known as personal banks or consumer banks. These are the banks where people in the community deposit their money. Retail banks also provide loans for homes, cars, education, and more.

Commercial banks, on the other hand, are usually used by corporations, or businesses, and governments. They provide many services similar to those of retail banks. Customers can deposit and borrow money, for example. But commercial banks may also offer other services specifically for businesses.

There are about 25,000 commercial banks in the world.

The United States has more banks than any other country.

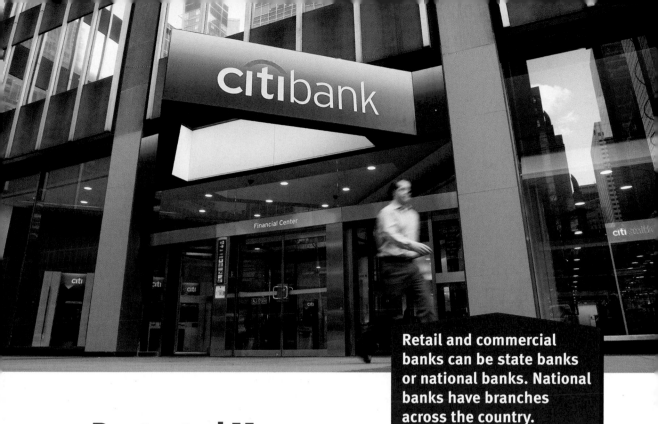

Protected Money

Nearly all banks in the United States are protected by the Federal Deposit Insurance Corporation (FDIC). This government entity provides insurance to banks. So if the bank fails, depositors won't lose their money. FDIC insurance covers up to $250,000 per account. Most countries around the world offer a similar type of deposit protection.

The three largest banks in the United States are J.P. Morgan Chase & Co., Bank of America, and Wells Fargo & Co.

Customers need a personal identification number (PIN) to use an ATM.

Checking Accounts

Most American adults have a deposit account. That is an account where they can deposit their money. They can also **withdraw** money from the account. A checking account is one type of deposit account. That is a good place to store money that needs to be accessed regularly—to pay bills or buy groceries, for example. Checking accounts come with **checks** and a **debit card**. Account holders can make withdrawals to pay for items by writing a check or using their debit card. They can also use their debit card at an automated teller machine (ATM) to take cash from their account.

The Federal Reserve

The Federal Reserve System, also called the Fed, is the central bank of the United States. There are 12 banks in the system, each serving a different part of the country. The Fed is different from other banks in that it doesn't serve customers directly. Each bank oversees the retail and commercial banks in its region. Among other things, the Fed sets the base **interest** rate, which is also called the federal funds rate. The federal funds rate influences the interest rates set by individual banks. For example, if the Fed raises rates, banks will too.

Interest rates are shown as percentages. That means the rate is proportional to the amount of money it applies to.

This building houses the headquarters of the Federal Reserve in Washington, D.C.

Savings Accounts

A savings account is another type of deposit account. Unlike with a checking account, money in a savings account is not for everyday use. It is usually being put aside for the future. Savings accounts allow you to deposit money and earn interest, which is a payment for the use of your funds. Different accounts have different interest rates. As you read on page 13, those rates are influenced by the base interest rates set by the Federal Reserve.

Imagine a savings account pays you a 5% annual interest rate on your money. If you deposit $100, after a year you will have $105.

Piggy banks do not pay interest. That is one reason why it is probably better to keep money in a real bank. What is another reason?

"What interest does a piggy bank pay?"

There are different types of savings accounts. In a traditional savings account, the interest rate is usually not very high. Customers have an advantage, though—they can easily withdraw the money they deposited. Other types of savings accounts offer higher interest rates, but they have stricter rules. Some require a minimum deposit. Others require the customer to keep the money in the account for a certain amount of time—typically from three months to five years.

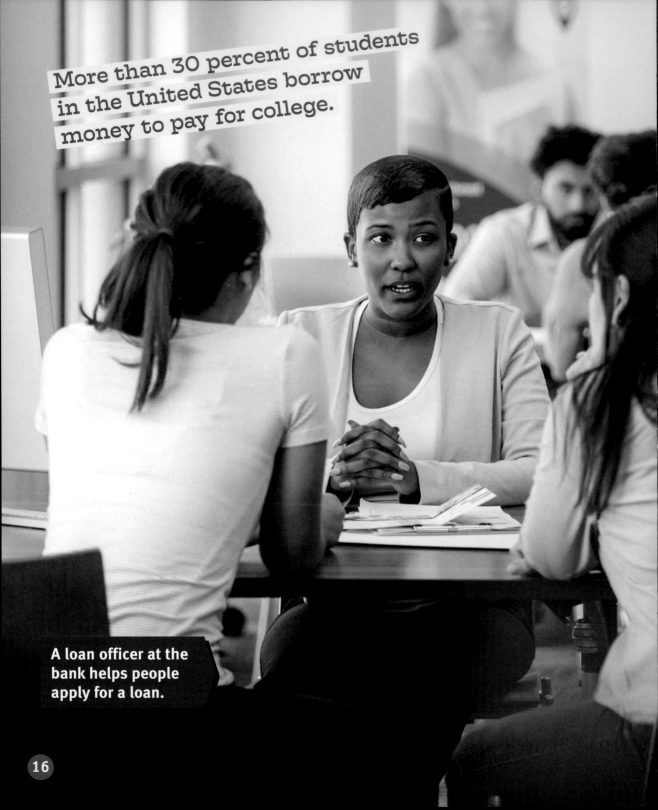

More than 30 percent of students in the United States borrow money to pay for college.

A loan officer at the bank helps people apply for a loan.

Borrowing from the Bank

Banks use the money customers have in deposit accounts to make loans to other customers. Banks cannot loan out all of their money, though! They are required to hold a certain amount of cash on hand for when customers come to the bank to make a withdrawal.

When banks loan money to someone, the person is expected to pay that money back. The borrower must also pay interest. That is one way the bank makes money.

Loan Basics

When people borrow money from a bank, they must agree on a few things: how much money they will borrow; what the interest rate will be; and the **term**, or when they will be expected to pay the loan back in full. Loans that are to be paid back within one year or less are called short-term loans. A loan that lasts longer than one year is a long-term loan. Many personal loans, student loans, car loans, and home loans are examples of long-term loans.

Timeline of the History of Banks

2000 BCE TO 310 BCE
In Greece, Rome, Babylon, and Egypt, temples are used as the first banks—a safe place for people to keep their money and get loans.

310 BCE
During the Roman Empire, banks become buildings separate from temples.

1600s AND 1700s
Merchant banks are established in France to finance business activities.

1791
Alexander Hamilton establishes the First Bank of the United States, the country's first central bank.

Personal Loans and Student Loans

Personal loans can be used for anything—like a vacation or a wedding. They typically have to be paid within two to seven years. Many people have to take out a student loan to pay for college. A private student loan comes from a bank. A federal student loan comes from the U.S. government. Federal loans often have lower interest rates and **defer** payment until graduation. The same might not always be true for a loan from a bank.

1967
The first automated teller machine (ATM) debuts in north London. Two years later, the first ATM opens in America.

1994
The Stanford Federal Credit Union in California is the first to offer online banking.

2005
Direct banks (banks that operate without physical offices) offer online-only services to customers.

2022
Nearly two-thirds of the people in the United States use digital banking applications.

A new car costs more than $15,000.

Car Loans and Home Loans

People often have to take out loans for very expensive purchases, like cars and homes. These loans are secured loans, which means they are backed by the thing that is being purchased. If the borrower fails to make loan payments, the bank will take ownership of the car or the home. Car loans typically range from 36 to 84 months. A home loan, also called a mortgage, can have up to a 30-year term.

Fixed or Variable?

Interest rates on loans can be fixed or variable. A fixed interest rate means the rate will stay the same for the entire term of the loan. A variable interest rate means the rate can change. Someone might choose a variable rate if they think rates will go down in the near future. Variable rates are also typically good for people who are planning to keep their home for a short time only, because the initial interest rates are often lower than with fixed-rate mortgages.

In the United States, the lowest mortgage rate to date was 2.65 percent in January 2021.

More than 60 percent of homeowners in the United States have a mortgage.

The woman in this cartoon has charged as much as she can to her credit card. She has reached her card's limit. Based on what you've learned, do you think a person can get a credit card "refilled"?

Give Me Credit!

A credit card is like a loan in that a person can buy something today and not have to pay for it until the next month. That makes a credit card different from a debit card. When you use a debit card, the money comes out of your account immediately. And all you can spend is the money you have. On the other hand, with a credit card you are spending money you might not have. You have to pay it back. And if you don't pay the full amount when the credit card bill comes, you will be charged interest on the amount still owed.

How Interest Rates Affect People's Actions

When interest rates are low, people are more likely to take out loans for bigger purchases, like a car or a house. Because borrowing is cheap, people are more inclined to spend more money in stores. When businesses do well, firms hire more employees. These workers now have money to spend too. All these things strengthen the country's economy. When interest rates are high, on the other hand, people are less likely to take out loans. People put more money into savings and spend less. This slows the economy down.

Paying Back a Loan

Every loan is different, but in general, loan payments are structured so that the borrower pays a certain amount every month until the loan is paid off. The amount the person pays each month includes **principal**, which is the original amount borrowed, and interest. That is a standard repayment plan. There are other types of payment plans for different types of loans.

Student loans often have more flexibility in payment plans than other loans do.

A loan statement shows how much principal and interest you'll pay every month.

AMORTIZATION SCHEDULE FOR MONTHLY PAYMENTS

Period	Regular payment	Interest paid	Principle paid	End balance
1	942.70	208.33	734.37	
2	942.70	206.80	735.90	99265.63
3	942.70	205.27	737.43	98529.74

LOANS

SCHWADRON

"HOW DO I KNOW YOU'LL STILL BE AROUND IN A YEAR?"

This cartoon illustrates one concern that banks have about loaning money. They have to trust that the borrower will pay it back! Do you think the banker would give a snowperson a short-term loan or a long-term loan?

Tips for Paying Off a Loan

The interest a borrower pays on a loan is a percentage of the loan amount. So it makes sense that borrowers should try to reduce the money they owe as quickly as possible! They can do that by making extra payments in addition to their scheduled payment whenever possible. They can also add extra money to each payment.

How Do Banks Make Money?

Banks play an important role in keeping our economy strong and helping people achieve their goals. But a bank is a business—and it is in business to make money. So if banks are always either protecting our money or giving it away, how do they make a **profit**?

THE NET INTEREST SPREAD

Banks receive interest from loans, and they pay out interest on deposit accounts. The net interest spread is the difference between the two. For example, if a bank is charging 7 percent interest on loans and paying 3 percent interest on deposits, the net interest spread is 4 percent. That is the bank's profit. And that is why the interest paid on a deposit will never equal or be greater than the interest charged on a loan.

FEES

Banks also make money by charging their customers for certain services.

MAINTENANCE FEE: This is a monthly fee that customers pay to have an account with a bank.

OUT-OF-NETWORK ATM FEE: Customers may be charged for taking cash out of an ATM that isn't part of their bank's network.

OVERDRAFT FEE: Banks charge a fee when a customer writes a check for more money than is in the account.

PAPER STATEMENT FEE: Some banks that send customers paper statements every month charge for the service. Customers who view their statements online instead can avoid this fee.

Thanks to all these gains, banks are very profitable businesses! In fact, as of June 30, 2022, more than 95 percent of all banks showed profitability. In contrast, only about 40 percent of small businesses are able to turn a profit.

More than 55 percent of American adults invest in stocks.

Between 500 and 1,000 people work on the floor of the New York Stock Exchange.

Investments

Imagine that someone gives you a significant amount of money for your birthday or another special occasion. But there's one catch: You can't spend the money until you graduate from high school. What's the best way for your money to grow? You will earn interest if you put the money into certain savings accounts. Your money will probably grow at a relatively steady rate. However, you might want to **invest** that money instead! An investment banker, who might work for your bank, can help!

"I take it your portfolio is doing well?"

Risky Business

You will invest that money if you want to have the opportunity to get a higher rate of return. That means that if your investment does well, you will make a lot more money than you would from the interest on your savings account. But the opposite is also true. If the investment does poorly, you could lose money. Investing can be very risky!

Find Your Balance

Usually, the riskier an investment is, the better chance there is for a high rate of return. An investment banker can help people find the right balance between risk and reward. There are a few common investment options available, such as stocks, bonds, and mutual funds. Let's explore them!

People usually do a lot of research before making an investment.

Phone apps allow investors to keep an eye on their investments.

Investing in Stocks

Purchasing stocks is a way to invest in a company. When a person buys a share of stock, they are getting a small piece of ownership in that company. Then they earn a portion of the company's profits. To make money, people try to buy stocks at a low price and sell them at a high price. Buying stocks can be a risky investment but also provides the opportunity for high returns.

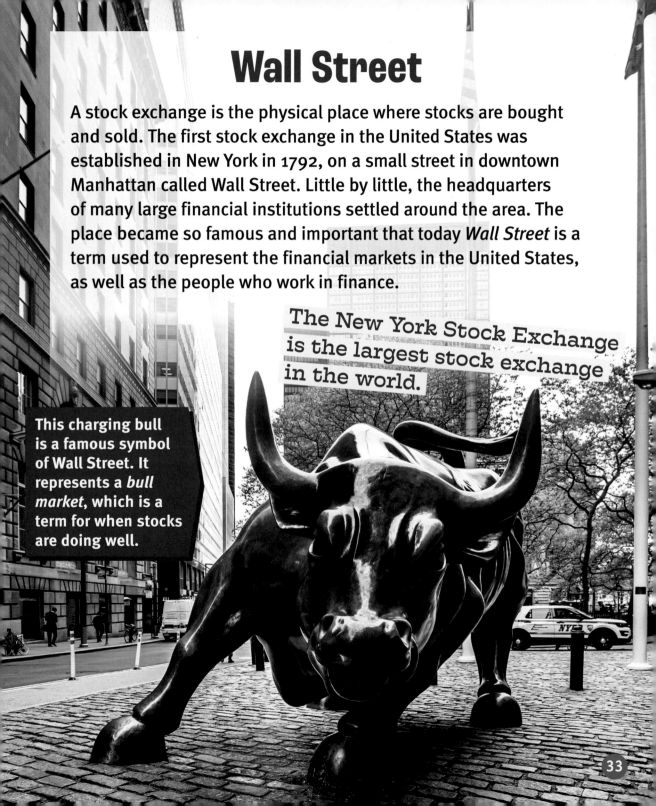

Wall Street

A stock exchange is the physical place where stocks are bought and sold. The first stock exchange in the United States was established in New York in 1792, on a small street in downtown Manhattan called Wall Street. Little by little, the headquarters of many large financial institutions settled around the area. The place became so famous and important that today *Wall Street* is a term used to represent the financial markets in the United States, as well as the people who work in finance.

The New York Stock Exchange is the largest stock exchange in the world.

This charging bull is a famous symbol of Wall Street. It represents a *bull market*, which is a term for when stocks are doing well.

Picking a Stock

It is important to do some research before picking a stock. An investment banker can help with that too! First, it is important to try to predict the stock's future performance by seeing how it performed in the past. Then you and your banker should also find out how well the company does compared to other companies in the same industry. For example, you probably wouldn't want to invest in a company that consistently lost money!

Companies are required to file financial reports every year. Those are good research tools.

Investing in Bonds

A bond is a loan that an investor is making to a business or government. In return, the company or government promises to pay the investor a specified rate of interest throughout the life of the bond. That interest is usually paid every six months. The

The United States issued bonds in 1941 to help pay for World War II.

company or government also promises to repay the principal when the bond's term ends. Bonds are considered a less risky investment than stocks because they provide a steady income stream. Investors still need to be careful because there is a possibility that the borrower can default, or be unable to pay off the bond.

The ratio of risky to safe investments in a mutual fund is up to the investor.

Mutual Funds

Mutual funds are created and managed by financial experts called fund managers. These investments are **diversified**. They contain a variety of different **assets**, including stocks and bonds. That makes mutual funds a relatively low-risk investment. Even if one asset doesn't perform well, other assets within the mutual fund will likely offset that result.

Education Plans

This investment is specifically designed to save money for education costs. A common education plan is the 529 plan. The money in a 529 is typically invested in a mutual fund or similar investment that will help it grow over time. Another advantage of investing in an education plan is that you don't have to pay taxes on the money you make—as long as it is used for education.

After years of study & hard effort, you're ready to begin your life's work...

About 15 million American families have invested in 529 education plans.

Chalkowski

...paying off your student loan.

This cartoon speaks to how expensive it is to go to college—and how many students have to take loans. How do you think investing in a 529 plan would impact this?

Retirement Plans

Many people begin saving for retirement—or when they will stop working—several years ahead of time. Two popular retirement plans are individual retirement accounts (IRAs) and employee-sponsored retirement plans, such as a 401(k). In both cases, a person's money is invested in a variety of assets.

About 75 percent of Americans have some type of retirement savings.

A retirement plan is an important source of income for a retired person.

Banks and the Economy

A bank is a very profitable business. It is also an important part of a community. A bank is a place where people can keep their money safe—and even watch it grow. It is also a

It feels great to see your money grow!

place that can help people reach their goals—such as owning a home, starting a business, making investments, or getting a college education. And by providing these services, banks play a big part in keeping the nation's economy strong.

Interest Rates over Time

Below is a graph that shows base interest rates in the United States as set by the Federal Reserve from 1970 to 2022. Study the graph and answer the questions.

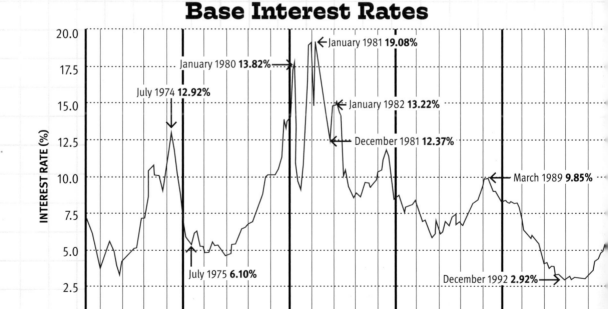

Base Interest Rates

July 1974 **12.92%**

January 1980 **13.82%**

January 1981 **19.08%**

January 1982 **13.22%**

December 1981 **12.37%**

March 1989 **9.85%**

July 1975 **6.10%**

December 1992 **2.92%**

INTEREST RATE (%)

YEAR

Analyze It!

1 At what point(s) were interest rates lowest?

2 At what point(s) were interest rates highest?

3 In what one-year period did the greatest change (up or down) occur? How much did the interest rate go up or down in that period?

4 When would have been the best time to lock in a fixed-rate mortgage?

ANSWERS: 1. May 2020; **2.** January 1981; **3.** July 1974 to July 1975; the rate fell by 6.82 percentage points; **4.** May 2020

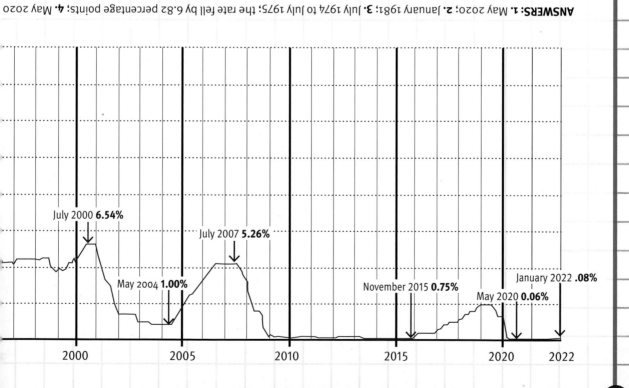

July 2000 **6.54%**

July 2007 **5.26%**

May 2004 **1.00%**

November 2015 **0.75%**

January 2022 **.08%**

May 2020 **0.06%**

2000   2005   2010   2015   2020   2022

Play the Stock Market!

Imagine you have $1,000 to invest in the stock market. Ask an adult to help you research two companies to invest in. Then look up the performance of both stocks over the past year.

Materials

Paper

Marker or pen

Internet

Directions

1 On a piece of paper, use a marker or pen to draw a T-chart like the one on the following page. Write the name of each company you chose in the appropriate column.

2 Use a trusted online resource to look up how much each stock cost one year ago today. This is your purchase price per share. Fill that in on the chart. How many shares of each company could you have bought with your $1,000? Add that information to the chart.

3 Now research the stock price from your start date up to today. Write down the price for the same date in each month.

STOCK MARKET PERFORMANCE

Company #1 _____   Company #2 _____

Purchase price per share: _____   Purchase price per share: _____

Number of shares: _____   Number of shares: _____

Stock Price per Month

$ _____ in _____
$ _____ in _____
$ _____ in _____
$ _____ in _____
$ _____ in _____
$ _____ in _____
$ _____ in _____
$ _____ in _____
$ _____ in _____
$ _____ in _____
$ _____ in _____
$ _____ in _____

Stock Price per Month

$ _____ in _____
$ _____ in _____
$ _____ in _____
$ _____ in _____
$ _____ in _____
$ _____ in _____
$ _____ in _____
$ _____ in _____
$ _____ in _____
$ _____ in _____
$ _____ in _____
$ _____ in _____

4 How did the stocks perform over time? Did they go up or down in value? Did they grow or decline steadily or abruptly?

5 Ask your adult to help you figure out what would have happened to your $1,000 investment in both companies. Which company would have given you a better rate of return?

True Statistics*

Number of commercial banks in the United States: About 4,500

First bank founded in the United States: Philadelphia's Bank of North America, in 1781

Percentage of adults in the United States who don't have a bank account: 7 percent

Number of people in the United States with a personal loan: 20.4 million

Percentage of homeowners in the United States with a mortgage loan: Approximately 64.8 percent

Note: These statistics are as of 2022.

Did you find the truth?

T Banks earn money by making loans.

F Stocks are low-risk investments.

Resources

Other books in this series:

You can also look at:

Andal, Walter. *Finance 101 for Kids: Money Lessons Children Cannot Afford to Miss*. Columbus, OH: Gatekeeper Press, 2016.

Baby Professor. *All About Banks*. Newark, DE: Speedy Publishing, 2017.

Bair, Sheila. *Rock, Brock, and the Savings Shock*. Park Ridge, IL: Albert Whitman, 2017.

Glossary

assets (AS-ets) valuable things that a person or business owns

checks (CHEKS) printed pieces of paper on which someone writes to tell the bank to pay a specific amount of money from their account to another person or to a company

debit card (DEB-it KAHRD) a plastic card that is connected to a bank account and that can be used to pay for things

defer (di-FUR) to postpone until later

deposit (di-PAH-zit) to put money into a bank account

diversified (di-VUR-si-fyed) made up of varied products

economy (i-KAH-nuh-mee) the system of buying, selling, making things, and managing money in a place

interest (IN-trist) a fee paid for borrowing money, usually a percentage of the amount borrowed, as well as money paid to you by a bank for keeping your savings there

invest (in-VEST) to give or lend money to something, such as a company, with the intention of getting more money back later

principal (PRIN-suh-puhl) the amount a person borrows

profit (PRAH-fit) the amount of money left after all the costs of running a business have been subtracted from the money earned

term (TURM) a definite or limited period of time

withdraw (with-DRAW) to take money out of an account

Index

Page numbers in **bold** indicate illustrations.

About the Authors

Janet Liu (top) and Melinda Liu (bottom) are sisters who are passionate about economic and financial literacy for young people. They are the founders of the nonprofit organization J&M Sunrizon Economics and the creators of the Wonderland Economics YouTube channel. Janet and Melinda are also the authors of *Elementary Economics* and *Economics for Tweens*, and are currently undergrads studying economics, computer science, and management at the Massachusetts Institute of Technology (MIT).